1 THESSALONIANS

LIVING FOR JESUS

10 Publishing
a division of 10 of those.com

1 THESSALONIANS: Living for Jesus

Published 2012

Published by 10Publishing, a division of 10ofthose.com
Unit 19 Common Bank Industrial Estate, Ackhurst Road, Chorley, PR7 1NH
Email: info@10ofthose.com
Website: www.10ofthose.com

British Library Cataloguing in Publication Data.
A catalogue record for this book is available from the British Library.

ISBN: 978-1-906173-67-8

Cover Design and Typeset by: Diane Bainbridge
Printed by: www.printbridge.co.uk

Julia Marsden

30 UNDATED DEVOTIONS THROUGH THE BOOK OF 1 THESSALONIANS

INTRODUCTION

Becoming a Christian is the beginning of a whole new relationship.

There are lots of wonderful things about becoming a Christian. We come to know God as our loving heavenly Father. We have a new family on earth, made up of all our Christian brothers and sisters. We have forgiveness for all our rebellion against God – for everything that is wrong in our lives, everything that separates us from Him. We need not fear death any more. We know the truth about life, death, God and what we are here for.

Jesus Christ died to make all this possible. He died in our place to take the punishment we deserve. And now Jesus calls us to trust Him and live under His loving rule. To become a Christian is to come to see who Jesus is and why He came, and to begin to trust and obey Him.

At the heart of all that happens when we become Christians is the wonder of being given a new relationship with the God who made us. God adopts us into His own family as His dearly loved children. Now we can call the creator of the whole universe our Father. God sends His Spirit to live in our hearts. His Spirit assures us that we are now in God's family. He helps us to live in a way that pleases our heavenly Father.

How are we going to live in this new relationship? How will we know what pleases our Father? How can we learn to listen to Him?

Communication is vital in any relationship, and no less in our new relationship with God. God speaks to us through His Word, the Bible. That is why reading the Bible is such a vital part of keeping going and growing in the Christian life. As we read the Bible we are reading God's words. The Bible is God speaking to us.

This booklet will help you read through one short book of the Bible in thirty days.

Each day's notes include some questions. You will find the answers in the part of the Bible we are looking at that day. There is a space in the notes for you to write your answers if you would like to. Sometimes you will find an extra section to read if you wish. These extra sections explain a bit more about something mentioned in the day's reading.

Reading the Bible is not an end in itself. We read the Bible so we can get to know God better and come to love Him more. We need to listen to His voice so we can learn what will please Him.

God speaks to us through His Word. How should we respond? We need to respond by talking to God about what we hear. We also need to take action to change. Ask God to help you as you read each day, and talk to Him about what you are learning. You will find some suggestions for prayer at the end of each day's notes.

Julia Marsden

READ 1 Thessalonians 1:1

The Bible book we are going to read is a letter written about twenty years after Jesus' death and resurrection. It was written to a group of new Christians. They lived in Greece in a city called Thessalonica. They had heard the message about Jesus, and had decided to follow Him. Perhaps you too are new to following Jesus.

Paul and his friend Silas (who is sometimes called Silvanus) had brought the message about Jesus to Thessalonica. Then Paul and Silas had had to leave. A short time later, this letter arrived in Thessalonica.

- ***Have a look at the first verse. Who was writing this letter?***

- ***Who were they writing to?***

- ***What does this verse tell us about where these Christians lived?***

So, Paul and his co-workers were writing to these new Christians. As we read on, we will see that they wanted to encourage these new believers to keep going in the Christian life. They also wanted to reassure them in the face of the doubts and difficulties that had come their way.

- ***What is that little word 'in' telling us?***

Paul, Silas and Timothy are writing to 'the church of the Thessalonians in God the Father and the Lord Jesus Christ'. That little word 'in' tells us something very important about what happens when you become a Christian.

It tells us that when you become a Christian, you become someone who lives in two places. This gathering of Christians ('church' just means gathering) were Thessalonians; they lived in Thessalonica. But whether you live in Thessalonica or Tewkesbury or Tennessee, if you are a Christian you also live somewhere else. You also live 'in God the Father and the Lord Jesus'.

What does that mean? It means that you are now as close to God as it is possible to get. Wherever you are – on the bus, in the kitchen, at work, wherever – you are close to God and secure in Him, whatever else happens to you. You are united to God in a way that nothing can destroy.

That's a great thought to take with you into your day and to thank God for.

- ***What did Paul and his co-workers want for this church?***

Because of what Jesus had done for them on the cross, God's grace had come to these Thessalonians. They, like every Christian, had received God's free forgiveness for all their sins, all their rebellion against God. So now they were at peace with Him. We too share this wonderful experience. God is no longer distant from us. He is right there with us, all the time, and will be every day. Forever.

Paul and his friends wanted these new believers in Thessalonica to keep going as Christians. He wanted them to keep enjoying grace from God and peace with God, and peace with each other too. This letter would encourage them to do just that. Pray that this letter would help you, too, to keep living in the grace and peace of God.

PRAY

- ***Thank God that you now live 'in God the Father and the Lord Jesus Christ'.***
- ***Thank God that you have experienced God's grace through trusting Jesus.***
- ***Pray that this letter would help you to keep knowing God's grace and peace.***

A WORD ABOUT CHURCH

This letter was written to a church. The word 'church' in the Bible never refers to a physical building. It always means a gathering of Christians. God's plan is that everyone who follows Jesus should be part of a local gathering of believers.

When God adopts us into His family, He brings us into a whole range of new relationships. We come to know God as our heavenly Father. We also find that every other believer is in this family with us. They are our spiritual brothers and sisters. We need their love, support and encouragement, and they need ours. Following Jesus is not something God wants us to do on our own.

It may be that you haven't joined a local church fellowship yet. How should you choose which one to join?

Becoming a Christian means that you now trust Jesus as your Saviour and want to follow Him as your Lord. So you will need to know what He wants you to do. The way we do that is by listening very carefully to His Word, the Bible. So, find a church which is teaching the Bible. When you visit, see what happens in the sermon or talk. Does the preacher or teacher carefully explain what is in the Bible? Is the congregation encouraged to open a Bible during the sermon or talk and look at it carefully? If they are, that is a very good sign!

You also want to find a church which welcomes and supports you, and where you can serve others. Is there a Bible study group you can join? That will be a very helpful way of learning and getting to know a small group of Christians really well.

Lastly, find a church where you would be happy to bring someone who is not yet a Christian. We want those we know to find out about Jesus too. Is the good news about Jesus as Saviour and Lord clearly explained at the church? Is it a place which is easy to come to? If you find what goes on at the church embarrassing, strange or off-putting, probably your friend would too.

Choose your church with care. Make meeting with your church family a priority. Don't miss out on being there to hear God's Word explained, and to encourage each other. You need them, and they need you. God doesn't want you to be on your own.

Just before we read on in our letter, let's see what we can find out about these new Christians in Thessalonica. After all, this is a personal letter which was written to them in the first place. Knowing about them and their situation will help us understand the letter better.

Other parts of the Bible often help us understand the particular part we are reading. Another book in the Bible called Acts tells us how some of the first churches began. So reading Acts can often help us understand the letters which were written to these churches later on. That is certainly true of the church in Thessalonica. Today we read the account from the book of Acts of how the message about Jesus first came to Thessalonica.

- ***What happened during Paul's visit to Thessalonica?***

Paul and his friends arrived in the city. They went to the Jewish synagogue and started speaking about Jesus Christ. They went there on three different weeks to do this. Some people wanted to become Christians. Others were furious. As a result, Paul's opponents caused a riot in the city. Some of these new Christians had a terrible time. Paul and Silas had to leave town under cover of night. The Christians encouraged them to go, seemingly for Paul and Silas' own safety.

- ***What did Paul do when he was in the synagogue in Thessalonica? (Look carefully at the words used to describe what Paul did.)***

He 'reasoned... from the Scriptures', 'explaining', 'proving', 'proclaiming', and 'persuaded'.

Words, words, words.

If you had been watching Paul, you would have seen him doing a lot of talking – lots of words coming out of his mouth.

- ***What was the heart of his message?***

Paul was telling them about Jesus' death and resurrection. He was explaining and proving that Jesus' resurrection showed that Jesus was God's chosen King (that is what 'Christ' means) (v.3).

- ***What was the result of all this reasoning and explaining?***

The message about Jesus always divides people. We can see that here in Thessalonica. There were two responses to what Paul said about Jesus:

1. Some were persuaded by his words and joined Paul (v.4). That is how people become Christians. You hear someone speaking words – words about Jesus. You hear someone explain that Jesus is Saviour and Jesus is Lord. In one sense it seems very ordinary, just words.

But what is going on when people speak about Jesus is far from ordinary. We will see that as we read Paul's letter. Words about Jesus have the power to transform lives. Words about Jesus can bring people rescue from God's judgement. But we need to respond to these words in the right way. In Thessalonica, some people did just that. Some people accepted Paul's message, and they became Christians too.

2. But others rejected the message and made trouble. There was violence against Christians – accusations, danger, opposition, persecution. Following Jesus will always provoke opposition and hostility from some. Perhaps you have already found that yourself.

Words about Jesus are very powerful.

- ***Who told you about Jesus and all He has done for you? Thank God that this message has come to you. Ask God to help you to be a sharer of it too, whatever the cost.***

- ***Who could you speak to? Pray for an opportunity to speak to that person about Jesus.***

Even if you have only been a Christian a very short time, you can say something to others about Jesus. You can tell others what you know of Him. If people ask you questions you can't answer, it's fine to say, 'I don't know, but I will find out.' But do say something, because words about Jesus are very powerful. They can transform people's lives.

PRAY

- ***Thank God that someone brought the message about Jesus to you and told you that Jesus is Lord and Saviour.***
- ***Ask God to give you opportunities and courage to speak to others about Jesus.***

DAY 3 You do have 'the real thing' – keep going

So, there had been a riot in Thessalonica. Paul and Silas had left town in a hurry. What had been going on since they left?

Have a look at these phrases from different parts of the letter:

> ***You know, brothers, that our visit to you was not a failure. (2:1)***
>
> ***But, brothers, when we were torn away from you for a short time (in person, not in thought), out of our intense longing we made every effort to see you. (2:17)***
>
> ***So when we could stand it no longer... We sent Timothy... to strengthen and encourage you in your faith, so that no-one would be unsettled by these trials... when we were with you, we kept telling you that we would be persecuted. And it turned out that way... when I could stand it no longer, I sent to find out about your faith. I was afraid... our efforts might have been useless. (3:1–5)***
>
> ***But Timothy has just now come to us from you and has brought good news about your faith and love... we were encouraged about you... we pray most earnestly that we may see you again and supply what is lacking in your faith. (3:6–10)***

- ***What can you piece together about what might have been going on?***

It seems that these new Christians had had a tough time. Trials had come. It may be that some people were saying that Paul's visit had been a failure. Maybe some were saying that the gospel Paul had brought wasn't the 'real McCoy'. After all, it had led to much suffering for these Christians. Was it really the genuine article? And wasn't Paul a bit dodgy too? Did he really care about these Christians? He had left in a hurry and never been back. Was he just a slick salesman feathering his own nest in some way?

Paul had heard that the Christians had been under pressure. He had been worried that they might have given up trusting in Jesus. But Timothy had just brought good news about them. These new believers hadn't given up. In fact, they were going on well as Christians.

Can you sense the huge relief Paul felt? He was thrilled. But now he wanted to keep building their faith more and more. He wanted to reassure them in the face of doubts and criticisms.

Do you sometimes wonder whether the message about Jesus is the real thing? Is it really what life is all about? Ask God to reassure you as you read this letter that it is just that. The Thessalonians suffered for being Christians. That may well be your experience too. But ask God to help you to keep growing in your faith, even when it's tough.

PRAY

- ***Talk to God about any doubts which are on your mind.***
- ***Ask God to use this letter to reassure you that the message about Jesus is true.***
- ***Ask God to help you grow in your faith even through sufferings.***

DAY 4

READ 1 Thessalonians 1:2,3

These new Christians in Thessalonica were keeping going in their faith in Christ, and Paul was delighted. So, he wrote to thank them for keeping going under so much pressure. Well, no. He didn't.

Have a look at verse 2. Who does Paul say thank you to here?

Paul knew that the Christian comitment of these believers was God's work – something to thank God for. So, whenever Paul prayed for them he thanked, not them, but God Himself.

- ***What does this tell you about your faith in Jesus?***

If you are a Christian today it is because God has saved you. That is a wonderful thing. But how has this happened? God did something for us at the cross of Jesus 2000 years ago. But God also does something in us today. God changes our hearts so that we want to love Jesus and follow Him. We need to thank God for both these things. When you see other people following Jesus, thank God, because you're looking at God's work, at something miraculous that God has done.

- ***What had Paul seen in his friends that made him thank God (v.3)?***

- ***What will God's work in someone actually look like?***

Paul said he could see 'work', 'labour' and 'endurance'. That was what was going on in the church in Thessalonica. People were active and working. They were keeping going under pressure. As someone has said, 'the sign of God at work is men and women at work'.

When God brings us to life spiritually, we begin to take action. We begin to make an effort to live to please God. We start to pray, to get rid of sin, to serve others, to speak about Jesus – all sorts of things.

Paul is going to expand on these things in chapters 4 and 5 of this letter. We're not saved by doing all these things. We are saved by what Jesus did for us on the cross. But a changed life is the evidence that we have been saved. It shows that God has changed us inside.

Later on in his letter, Paul will tell his friends to keep on making every effort to please God. Look at chapter 4 verse 1. The fact that God is at work in us doesn't mean we just lie back. We are to make every effort to please God more and more.

- ***What motivated these believers to make this effort? What motivated them to keep going as Christians even under pressure (v.3)?***

This work, labour and endurance came from their faith, love and hope in Jesus.

Their work sprang from their faith...
...their labour from their love...
...their endurance from their hope.

They had faith, love and hope in the Lord Jesus Christ.

To become a Christian is to change on the inside. In our hearts we begin to trust Christ, to love Him and to live with a certain hope. We now live looking forward to being with Christ forever in His new creation. But becoming a Christian brings more than just inward change. When we change on the inside it shows on the outside. We get busy serving Jesus, even if that is very costly.

Ask God to help you to keep trusting, loving and hoping in Christ so that you keep working to serve Him. Think about how you could work for Christ in your own church family or in your community. What could you do? Why not ask your church leader or a Christian friend for some ideas?

PRAY

- ***Thank God for the faith in Jesus you see in the lives of Christians you know.***
- ***Thank God for helping you trust, love and hope in Jesus.***
- ***Pray that those heart changes would make you into someone who works, labours and perseveres in serving Jesus.***
- ***Ask God to help you begin to serve your local church family.***

DAY 5

READ 1 Thessalonians 1:4–6

Knowing you are loved and wanted must be one of the greatest experiences of life. But knowing that you are loved and wanted by the God of the whole universe is in a class all by itself.

Do you know that this is true for you? Do you know that God has set His love on you? Do you know that God has put His hand on you and called you to be His own, to be with Him forever?

Paul said that he knew that those things were true of the believers in Thessalonica (v.4). But how did Paul know? How could he be so sure? Well, as we saw yesterday, Paul could see the work of God in their lives. His friends were now active in serving God. They were keeping going as Christians.

- ***But in today's verses Paul points to something else. What is it (v.5)?***

Paul pointed to how they had responded to the message about Jesus. If you had been at the synagogue the day Paul visited, what would you have seen? Just a man speaking words – words about Jesus. Some didn't like the message, but others responded differently.

Some were cut to the heart. They were convinced. They accepted Paul's message. They found that God Himself came into their lives. The Holy Spirit of God came to them in power. He changed them. He convicted them of their sin and their need of Christ.

- ***What is surprising about these Christians' joyfulness (v.6)?***

Becoming Christians had brought these believers great suffering, yet they were full of joy. They knew the joy of sins forgiven and the joy of knowing God. They began to want to be like Christ and His messengers. What a transformation!

On the surface it seemed that all they had done was accept words. But in accepting the message about Jesus, their whole lives had been changed. They had accepted the forgiveness and reconciliation that only Jesus can bring. They had been changed by the power of God, the Holy Spirit. Their response to the message showed that God had chosen them and that He loved them (v.4).

There is a great reassurance for us here. If we have accepted the message about Jesus, then we too can know that God has loved us and chosen us to be His own. If you responded in this way to the gospel, thank God for setting His love on you.

PRAY

- ***Thank God that you accepted the message about Jesus when you heard it.***
- ***Thank God for working in you by His Spirit to bring you to Himself.***
- ***Thank God for loving you and choosing you to belong to Him forever.***
- ***Pray that you would keep on accepting God's word with joy.***
- ***Pray that you would want to imitate Christ and His apostles.***

A WORD ABOUT GOD

In these first six verses of our letter we have read about God the Father (vv.1,3). We have read about the Lord Jesus Christ (vv.1,3,6). We have also read about the Holy Spirit (vv.5,6).

In the Bible, God reveals Himself to be a unity of three persons – the Father, the Son (the Lord Jesus Christ) and the Spirit. The Father is God. The Son is God. The Spirit is God. They have always existed together in a union of love.

The word Christians use to describe God is 'Trinity'. It means that God has revealed Himself to be one God in three persons. This tells us two very important things, one about God and the other about us:

1. God is, in Himself, a community of love. Father, Son and Spirit love each other perfectly and have done from all eternity. God did not make human beings because He was lonely and needed someone to love. God, in Himself, 'is love' (1 John 4:16). We would probably never have guessed that God is like this. But it is a wonderful truth.

2. The fact that God is, in Himself, a community of love, shows us a truth about ourselves. We have been made in God's image (Genesis. 1:26) and so we too are relational beings. That is why loneliness and broken relationships are so painful. That is why good friendships and happy families are so wonderful. We were made for relationships. Most of all, we were made for a relationship with God.

Through the gospel, God reaches out to us to draw us into His own loving community. God the Father, God the Son and God the Holy Spirit are all involved in working to rescue us, as we have already seen in these opening verses.

DAY 6

READ 1 Thessalonians 1:7–10

How does someone become a Christian?

We have seen over the last couple of days that it is God's work. We have also seen that it involves us hearing and accepting the message about Jesus. But what happens then? In verses 9 and 10, Paul gives us a great summary of what happens when someone does accept the message about Jesus.

- ***Becoming a Christian involves doing three things. What are they (vv.9,10)?***

- ***First, these people in Thessalonica had turned. What had they turned from (v.9)?***

What is an idol? An idol doesn't have to be a little gold statue. An idol is anything which takes God's place in your heart. First place in your life rightfully belongs to the God who made you and who gives you your every breath. If you give first place in your life to anything else, then that thing or that person becomes your idol.

For some people, their idol is status, money or success. For others it is self-image, health, pleasure or just selfishness. For others it might be family, sex or a particular relationship. Some people make an idea or ideology their idol.

Many of the things people make into idols are actually good gifts of God. But those things can become idols if we give them the top priority in our lives.

- ***What was your top priority before you became a Christian? What had first place in your heart?***

When we become Christians we change. We turn from idols.

If our idol was something sinful, we will need to stop pursuing it altogether. If our idol was something good in itself, then we need to change our priorities. We need to give God His rightful place. Idols must no longer have the number one place in our hearts. Ask God to help you keep turning away from your own idols.

- ***Secondly, the Thessalonians had begun to serve. Who did they serve now (v.9)?***

Instead of serving idols, these believers now served the living and true God. Their aim in life was now to please God and to put Him first in everything. Ask God to help you do that today.

- ***Thirdly, they were waiting. Who were they waiting for and why (v.10)?***

Becoming Christians had already brought these believers 'severe suffering' (v.6). As we read in Acts 17, some in their city were out to get them. People persecuted Jesus. People will persecute Christians, too. But the day is coming when God's full righteous anger (His 'wrath') against all sin and rejection of Jesus will be expressed. This is what Paul means by 'the coming wrath' (v.10). Jesus promised that He would return in glory as the Judge of all people, and on that day all sin and rebellion against God will be fully and justly punished.

For Christians, that day will be a great day. On that day all opposition to Christ and Christians will be destroyed. And on that day Christians will experience Christ's salvation. We will not have to face the wrath of God against our sin. Jesus Christ bore God's wrath against our sin when He died in our place. So on that last day we will meet Christ as forgiven sinners. Those who trust in Christ, and only those who trust Christ, have no need to fear that day.

To be a Christian is to live waiting for that great day. We live every day now in the light of what is coming then.

When we face persecution we need to remember that one day all opposition to God will be destroyed. Jesus' resurrection from the dead proves that He is Lord and Judge of all. And He is coming, not only as Judge of all, but also as our Saviour. Pray that you would live in the light of the coming of Christ as Judge and Saviour.

So, turning, serving, waiting: that is what it means to become a Christian. It begins in our hearts.

There is a change of allegiance. We turn from idols.

There is a new priority. We begin to serve God.

And there is a new perspective. We live waiting for Jesus' return.

Allegiance, priority, perspective – these are all changes in our hearts. It begins there, but it doesn't end there. Did you notice that Paul stresses over and over again in these verses that these changes have become public knowledge?

- ***What effect did the Thessalonians' faith have on others (vv.7,8)?***

Sometimes people say that they want their faith in Jesus to be a 'private thing'. But Christian faith is never a private matter in the Bible. It seems that the faith of these Thessalonian Christians had become big news. Lots of people were talking about what they were doing. Their lives had become a visual aid to the gospel. They were 'a model' (v.7) and a 'message' (v.8) from God Himself. Their lives were a tremendous encouragement to other Christians. But they were also a challenge to those who were not yet followers of Jesus.

If no one knows you are a Christian yet, do tell someone. Maybe tell a Christian friend first. They will be delighted. And pray that the message about Jesus would 'ring out' from the way you live now, to encourage Christians and help bring others to Christ.

PRAY

- ***Ask God to help you see what your idols have been.***
- ***Ask Him to help you keep turning away from them.***
- ***Ask God to help you keep serving Him until Jesus comes again.***
- ***Thank God that Jesus saves you from 'the coming wrath' which you deserve.***
- ***Pray that the message about Jesus would 'ring out' from your life.***
- ***Pray you would be able to tell someone that you have become a Christian.***

DAY 7

READ 1 Thessalonians 2:1–6

It's the real thing. It really is. This message about Jesus as Saviour and Lord is the real thing.

Paul was reassuring these new Christians that what had happened to them was God's work. The suffering and the hard graft that they were experiencing should not unsettle them. Those things did not mean they had got it all wrong. These believers would be safe on judgement day because of Jesus. It *was* worth it.

In today's passage, Paul reassures them about something else too. It may be that some people had been saying that these Christians had been duped. Perhaps questions were being asked. In deciding to follow Jesus, had these believers been taken for a ride? Had they been taken in by Paul? Wasn't Paul a manipulative salesman, a dodgy dealer just out for a fast buck?

Paul wanted to reassure them. He wanted to tell them about his own sincerity and integrity, and his genuine love for them. It's horrible to feel you've been conned about something, even something small. But how much worse to feel that you have changed the whole direction of your life on the basis of a con! Paul said it was not so.

- ***So, what were Paul's motives? That is the focus of today's verses. Why had Paul taken the message about Jesus to these Thessalonians?***

- ***What had gospel ministry been like for Paul? (Look at v.2.)***

Had bringing the gospel to people made Paul's life easy and comfortable? No. It had brought him a great deal of suffering. Why hadn't Paul and his friends given up? They hadn't given up because they had been given confidence and strength by God Himself ('with the help of our God', v.2).

- ***What does Paul say about his motivation for preaching the gospel in verses 3 to 6?***

Negatively, Paul had not been motivated by error, impurity, greed, or the desire to gain praise from people or please them. He had not been trying to flatter or trick them.

And positively? Look at how many times Paul refers to God in explaining his motivation for preaching. It was God's gospel (v.2). God had entrusted it to them and approved them to be sharers of it. They spoke in order to please God; God was the one who tested the genuineness of their hearts (v.4). And God was the witness of their sincerity (v.5). God, God, God. Paul's motivation was all about serving and pleasing God. He was not out to use, abuse or manipulate people.

Pray for those who lead and preach in your church that they would have the same integrity as Paul in the way they present the gospel to people.

Paul was personally appointed by Jesus to be His apostle (v.6). 'Apostle' means one who is sent. Jesus personally appointed particular people to be apostles – to preach and teach in His name and with His authority. The New Testament is the teachings of these apostles, written down either by the apostles themselves or their close associates. All the apostles were eyewitnesses of Jesus' resurrection.

It was very reassuring for the Thessalonians to know that Paul's ministry had total integrity. But it is very reassuring for us, too. Our faith in Christ rests on the apostles' witness and teaching as well. Thank God that we can have confidence in the integrity of those who wrote the Bible.

PRAY

- ***Thank God for the courage and integrity of Jesus' first apostles.***
- ***Thank God that we have the teachings of these apostles faithfully recorded in our New Testaments.***
- ***Pray that your church would preach the gospel with the same integrity as Paul.***
- ***Pray that your first motivation would be to please God rather than people.***

READ 1 Thessalonians 2:7,8

Paul loved God. That much was very clear from yesterday's verses. But did Paul really love the Thessalonians? Or had he just been 'doing a job' when he preached the gospel to them?

Paul had been wanting to reassure these Christians of his integrity. And there is more reassurance for them and for us in today's verses. Paul and his friends were not heartless, shady salesmen out to deceive and dupe the Thessalonians. In today's verses, Paul focuses on the real love that he and his friends had for the Christians in Thessalonica. Love is the hallmark of real Christian faith. Becoming a Christian brings us into genuine loving relationships – with God, and also with people.

- ***What had Paul and his friends shared with these Thessalonians (v.8)?***

- ***What impression do you get of Paul's relationship with them in these verses?***

Paul had shared the gospel message with these people (v.8). But he had not been like an impersonal delivery service, just getting a job done. He and his friends really cared about these Christians, and it showed. There is much for us to learn here about how we go about sharing the gospel and helping Christians grow.

These are lovely verses, full of warmth and affection. Look at the language Paul uses to describe the relationship he and his friends had with these Thessalonian Christians. They had 'loved [them] so much'. They had been 'gentle', 'like a mother caring for her little children'. They had shared their lives with them. Yes, these Christians really were 'so dear' to Paul and his friends.

Paul's care for these Christians may have been gentle, but it had not been weak or soppy. We know this because Paul's ministry among them had taken place in the midst of suffering and persecution, as we have already seen.

Paul and his friends really loved these people. And this love shaped the whole way they had behaved amongst them. The one flows from the other, doesn't it? It all begins in the heart. We saw yesterday that Paul shared the gospel because he wanted to please God. That was his heart's desire, so he hadn't used dodgy methods or pursued celebrity or riches for himself. And neither should we. We have seen authentic Christian ministry modelled in the life of Paul. It is a model we should copy today.

In today's verses, we have seen that Paul didn't just love God. He really loved the people he was speaking to as well. In fact, he had God's heart for them. He hadn't kept them at arm's length. He and his friends had shared their own selves with them.

There is always a big risk in doing that. You risk being hurt if you are rejected. But Paul said he had loved and cared for them like a mother does her little child. He longed to be with them. He longed for them to be safe and to grow. It was not 'just his job'.

The gospel is a message about God loving us and wanting to be close to us. Paul's life as well as his words had spoken this message to the Thessalonians. Pray that this would be true of our lives too.

PRAY

- ***Ask God to help you love Him and to love and care for others in the way we have been reading about.***
- ***Ask God to help you share the gospel and your own life with others, just as Paul did.***
- ***Thank God for those who have loved and cared for you in your church family.***

READ 1 Thessalonians 2:9–12

What helps you to keep going as a Christian?

It is a tremendous help to have people around you whom you trust. People whose example you want to follow. People who take time to encourage you individually.

As you read and think today, pray that God would give you people like that to help you. Thank Him if He already has. And pray that you would become someone like that for others too.

'You know us.' 'You remember how we lived among you, don't you?'

Yesterday, we looked at how Paul and his friends had shared their very selves with these Thessalonians. And all the way through these first two chapters, Paul uses the phrase 'you know...' or 'you remember...' See how many you can find. Paul kept on reminding these Christians of what they already knew first-hand about him and his ministry amongst them.

As we have seen, some may have doubted the integrity of Paul's ministry. But in today's verses, Paul reminds his friends of three more reassuring marks of his ministry:

- ***First, what does Paul say about his work (v.9)?***

Paul's point in verse 9 is that he had never asked the Thessalonians to pay him. He had never charged for preaching the gospel to them. And it wasn't because he was so rich he didn't need money. No. He and his friends had had to do ordinary work alongside their gospel ministry in order to live. They could have asked the Christians in Thessalonica for money (v.6) but they had chosen not to, not wanting to be a burden to them in any way.

- ***Secondly, how had Paul treated these Christians (v.10)?***

Paul was reminding them that the way he had treated them was always with Christian integrity. He had been holy, righteous and blameless (v.10). Paul and his friends hadn't been one thing in the pulpit and another when they were 'off-duty'. You can tell a false teacher not only by what they say but also by how they live. Paul is saying here that his life had backed up what he had taught.

- ***Thirdly, what had Paul actually done in his ministry amongst these believers (vv.11,12)?***

Paul reminded them that he had been like a father to them. Look at the words Paul used to describe his ministry: 'encouraging, comforting and urging'. All these terms have to do with speaking. Paul seems to have words in mind again here, doesn't he? As Paul spoke words to them, like a father, he gave each one individual help ('each of you', v.11). But his goal in all this was the same for each one – to help them 'live lives worthy of God' (v.12). That was what Paul had kept calling them to do.

What Paul wanted for them was exactly what God wanted for them. Did you notice that someone else was speaking to them too? Look at the end of verse 12. God Himself was calling these Christians to serve Him as their King forever. And Paul wanted them to do that too. So Paul kept speaking to each one – to encourage them and spur them on.

What could you say to another Christian this week that would encourage them to keep serving the Lord Jesus? Think about what others have said to you that you have found helpful. That will give you some ideas of how you might encourage someone else.

PRAY

- ***Thank God that He has called you into His own kingdom and glory.***
- ***Pray for those who lead your church.***
- ***Pray their lives would display Christian integrity and holiness at all times.***
- ***Pray that your leaders would encourage, comfort and urge each one to lead lives worthy of God.***
- ***Thank God for their hard work in doing this.***
- ***Ask God for an opportunity to speak to a Christian to encourage them, and for wisdom to know what you should say to each individual.***

DAY 10

READ 1 Thessalonians 2:13

How do I hear God speaking to me? It's an important question to think about.

Did you notice in the verses that we read yesterday that two people were speaking to the Thessalonians?

God was speaking to them ('God, who calls you').

And Paul and co. were also speaking to them ('encouraging, comforting and urging you').

- ***What does today's verse tell us about how God's word had come to these Christians?***

As Paul and his friends spoke, God Himself was speaking. Human words, yes. But not just human words.

God's word hadn't come to these Thessalonians through a voice speaking out of the sky. But as Paul had preached the gospel to them, they had recognised God speaking. God was calling them to repent and believe in Jesus. You can probably recognise that experience yourself. You read words in the Bible, or you have the Bible explained and preached to you, and you know that God Himself is speaking to you. Paul thanked God for this experience, and so should we. It is a sign of God at work in us.

So, Paul knew that his message about Jesus was God's word. It was God Himself speaking, God calling people to follow Jesus and to keep on following Him.

Do you remember a while back we were thinking about how Paul was one of Jesus' apostles? Jesus Himself appointed this special group of apostles to teach in His name. Right from the start, their writings were recognised as God's Word, as Scripture. Have a look at how Peter describes Paul's letters in 2 Peter 3 verses 15 to 16, for example.

What about today? Where do we find Jesus' apostles' teachings today? After all, we don't have Paul, John, Peter or any of Jesus' other apostles teaching in our churches. Today we hear Jesus' apostles speaking to us as we read the New Testament. The New Testament contains their teachings. God speaks to us today through the Bible. Words written by men, yes, but also words from God Himself.

- ***What does Paul say about what this Word of God does (v.13)?***

- ***How is God's Word 'at work' in us?***

In another of his letters Paul calls the Word of God 'the sword of the Spirit' (Ephesians 6:17). Paul means that God's Word is the instrument God's Spirit uses to help us in the Christian life. God's Spirit uses God's Word to protect us, challenge us, encourage us – all kinds of things. God's Word keeps us safe and keeps us going and growing as Christians. It transforms our lives and our characters – but only as we read it, hear it taught, think about it and humbly submit to it in our lives.

Hopefully you are doing those things now as you read the Bible on your own. But where else do you hear the Bible read and explained? At church. At a Bible study group. Studying with a Christian friend, maybe. We need to choose to do those things. It is vitally important that we do keep hearing and obeying God's Word. Let's pray we do, so that God's Word can do God's work in our lives as we listen and obey.

PRAY

- ***Thank God that you heard His voice calling you when you heard someone explaining the gospel.***
- ***Ask God to help you to keep treating the Bible as God's Word.***
- ***Thank God that His Word is 'at work' in you to transform you.***
- ***Ask God to help you keep choosing to listen to and obey His Word.***

DAY 11

READ 1 Thessalonians 2:14–16

How do you expect people will react to the news that you have become a Christian?

Your Christian brothers and sisters will be thrilled. Some who are not yet Christians may be interested in finding out about Jesus too. But there will be some people who won't like it at all and won't like you speaking about Jesus. Ask God to help you cope when this happens to you.

How will you cope? All the way through this first part of his letter, Paul was reassuring these new Christians. He was telling them that their Christian experience is genuine. He pointed them to the way they responded to the gospel and to the way their lives had changed as a result. He also pointed them to the trustworthiness of his own gospel ministry among them.

In today's verses, Paul points them to something else to reassure them. In verse 13 he assured them that God's word is 'at work' in them. And now he points them to one particular evidence of that work.

- ***What did these Christians do (v.14)?***

They copied the example of the churches in Judea. How did they do that? The Jewish churches had been willing to suffer for sharing the gospel. And these Thessalonian Christians did the same.

There is a big stress in these verses on the fact that this suffering for being a Christian is normal. Opposition to the gospel, and especially opposition from those close to home, is what we should expect. The Thessalonians and the Judeans both suffered persecution from their own countrymen. Jesus and the Old Testament prophets had the same experience. Their own people persecuted them. This remains the experience of many Christians today. Often it is those closest to us who cause us most grief for being Christians. Opposition may come from our family, our friends or our work colleagues. And that is so very, very painful.

So, Paul wanted to reassure these new believers that what was happening to them was normal Christian experience. They should not be thrown off course by the fact that this suffering had come to them.

Paul gave them two reasons to keep going, despite the suffering. Both have to do with God's wrath – that is, God's righteous anger against human sin.

- ***How can people be saved from God's wrath (v.16)?***

Paul reminded these Christians of the link between speaking the gospel and people being saved from God's wrath. It is only Jesus who can save us from God's wrath. This wrath is coming against our sin on the last day (1:10). But if people hear of Jesus and begin to trust and follow Him, they will be saved. So, keep going. Don't give up. Keep speaking to those who are willing to listen.

Paul had a Jewish background. And for Paul to minister amongst Gentiles (non-Jews) made him particularly unpopular. Jews then saw Gentiles as outsiders. But Paul knew that the message about Jesus was for everyone. We need to have the same conviction.

- ***How does God react to those who oppose gospel ministry and persecute Christians (vv.15,16)?***

Paul reminded his suffering friends that God is displeased with those who oppose the gospel (v.15). God sees all that is going on. These opponents would experience the wrath of God against their sins. Paul was so certain that this would happen he spoke of it as if it already had. He wanted to encourage his readers not to be scared of those who were making their lives so difficult.

People who oppose Christ may seem very powerful now. But one day their power will be gone. So don't be scared of them. We need to pray for courage to keep going and to keep speaking about Jesus, even when it brings suffering into our lives.

PRAY

- ***Pray that you would be willing to suffer for being a Christian and for sharing the gospel.***
- ***Ask God to help you remember that opposition, even from those closest to you, is part of normal Christian experience.***
- ***Thank God that the message about salvation through Jesus is for everyone.***
- ***Ask God to help you keep sharing this good news so that others might be saved too.***
- ***Ask God to help you not to be scared of those who persecute you.***
- ***Thank God that He sees what is going on and will bring His opponents to justice.***

DAY 12

READ 1 Thessalonians 2:17–20

Reassurance, reassurance and more reassurance. Reassurance has been Paul's theme. Paul gives his readers still more reassurance in today's verses.

Paul wanted these Christians to be in no doubt that their Christian experience was the real thing. He also wanted them to know that his love for them was genuine. We have seen that already. We do need lots of reassurance, especially when we are new to the Christian life. We need to know that it really is worth keeping going.

Now Paul goes on to reassure his readers about what he'd been doing after he'd left Thessalonica. Paul explains here what had happened next.

What had been going on with Paul and his friends since they'd left Thessalonica on the night of the riot? Had they forgotten all about the new Christians? After all, they'd left in a hurry and not been back.

- ***What had Paul been trying to do (v.17)?***

- ***Why?***

- ***What impression do you get of his feelings for these believers?***

- ***Why hadn't Paul succeeded in his plans (v.18)?***

In this next section of our letter (which runs from here up to 3:10), Paul tells the Thessalonians what has been going on.

He tells them how he had kept trying to come back to see them. But things hadn't worked out. He tells them how he had sent Timothy to find out how they were doing, and to encourage them. He tells them how Timothy had just returned with good news about them. Paul tells them of his own continued longing to see them again face to face. Paul's message is clear. He really does care about them.

Can you feel Paul's heartbeat for these Christians? He loved them so much. He hated being separated from them. Look at the dramatic and passionate language he uses to convey the depths of his love for them. He had felt 'torn away' from these Christians when he had left that night. It had been painful. His heart had remained with them in Thessalonica. '...out of [their] intense longing' Paul and his friends had tried again and again to come back, but had been prevented from doing so.

Paul does not say exactly what had stopped them, but he saw Satan's hand in it. Satan is always trying to disrupt gospel ministry.

- ***How do verses 19 and 20 help us understand why Paul was so bothered about this little bunch of Christians?***

Jesus is coming. We saw that in 1:10. And Jesus' coming changed the way Paul saw everything. It changed the way he saw those who opposed him, sharing the gospel (2:16), and it changed the way he saw other Christians too. Paul said that on the day he met Jesus, these Christians would be his 'hope', his 'joy', his 'glory' and his 'crown'.

- ***What did Paul mean?***

Well, what can you take with you into the new creation? Not money. Not possessions. But you can help to take people. We can share the gospel with others. We can help build them up in their faith.

What a tremendous privilege it is to be a part of someone's journey to be with Christ forever! It will be a very great joy to have them with us on that day. Pray you would see other Christians in the way Paul does here.

PRAY

- ***Thank God that Jesus is coming and that you will be part of the new creation He will bring.***
- ***Thank God that you will be with the rest of God's family on that day.***
- ***Ask God to help you care as deeply for your fellow Christians as Paul did.***
- ***Ask God to help you see Christians from this eternal perspective.***
- ***Ask God to help you do all you can to meet with them and encourage them to keep going.***

DAY 13

READ 1 Thessalonians 3:1–5

Being a Christian is not a picnic. It is a battle. And we need to stay alert and keep safe.

Paul and Silas had tried again and again to visit their friends in Thessalonica. But Satan had 'stopped' them. This probably doesn't mean that Paul had seen Satan standing in the middle of the road. But Paul was aware that Christians are involved in a spiritual battle. There are unseen powers of evil trying to stop God's work. Satan will use whatever means he can to hinder gospel ministry and to tempt Christians into giving up their faith.

That is one reason why we need to keep praying. We need to ask God to help us keep going in this battle. The idea of Satan opposing God's work sounds scary. But we can be assured that God is in control and that He will help us.

What did Paul and Silas do in the face of these setbacks? Did they give up? No, they thought of an alternative way to encourage these new believers.

- ***What did Paul and Silas do (v.2)?***

- ***What did they want Timothy to do (vv.2,5)?***

- ***What were Paul and Silas concerned about (vv.3,5)?***

So, Paul and Silas sent Timothy to Thessalonica. Twice Paul says, 'when we [or I] could stand it no longer' (vv.1,5). Paul did everything he could to help these young Christians. If one avenue closed up, he found another. He couldn't bear not to help them.

What was Paul worried about? He was concerned that his 'efforts' amongst them might have been 'useless' (v.5). He feared that his Thessalonian friends might give up following Jesus.

Why might they give up? Look at verse 3 and verse 5. Life sounds very tough for these believers, doesn't it? Trials. Persecution. Satan's 'the tempter' temptations.

In fact, suffering and temptation often do go together in Christian experience. You encounter suffering and there is always a temptation to move away from trusting God, to let trials 'unsettle' your faith (v.3).

What did Paul do in the face of these fears? We can see two things here.

- ***What did Paul remind them of in verse 3b and verse 4?***

Again and again in this letter Paul reminded his friends that suffering is normal for Christians. It is what all Christians should expect (notice all the 'we's in vv.3,4). Paul had already made this clear to them. 'You know quite well that...', Paul said (v.3). '... we kept telling you that...', he said (v.4).

Suffering does not mean that you have fallen out of God's hands. So, when bad things happens to you, run to God, not away from Him. Don't give up trusting Him. Ask God to help you keep trusting Him when tough things happen to you.

What else did Paul do? He feared these new believers might be thrown off course by these trials. So he sent Timothy, God's co-worker, to build up their faith. Do you see that in verse 2? Paul did not send Timothy to just give them tea and sympathy. God was at work in these believers through His word (remember 2:13?) and now Timothy was going to help in this work. Timothy would remind and teach them of all God had said and done for them. That would help them to stand firm in their faith, whatever happened.

How can you keep safe spiritually when you are under pressure? Keep listening to God's Word. Keep going to places where Christians will teach you God's Word and encourage you to persevere.

When things are tough, you may be tempted to stop going to church or to your Bible Study group. But these are the times when you will be most in need of the encouragement and teaching of other Christians.

Thank God for people who have been like Timothy in your own life. Ask God to help you learn to strengthen other people's faith through teaching them God's Word.

PRAY

- ***Ask God to help you say no to Satan's temptations to give up being a Christian.***
- ***Thank God for those who take time to teach you God's Word and encourage you.***
- ***Ask God to help you grow stronger in your faith in Him.***
- ***Ask God to help you stay close to Him in times of suffering.***
- ***Ask God to help you learn to strengthen the faith of others.***

DAY 14

READ 1 Thessalonians 3:6–10

Imagine someone has just returned from visiting some old friends of yours. What would you most want to hear news about? New babies? New jobs? Exciting holidays?

Today's verses are all about the news Timothy had just brought Paul about the Thessalonians.

What news had Paul just received about his friends (vv.6,8)?

It seems that the main focus of Paul's interest was the Thessalonians' 'faith and love' (v.6). How were they getting on in the Christian life? Were they 'standing firm in the Lord' (v.8), or had their faith collapsed?

As we saw a couple of days ago, Paul looked at these believers from an eternal perspective. He knew that the most important thing of all was staying as Christians. Ask God to help you have this eternal perspective about people you know too. In the end, whether or not we keep going as Christians is the thing that will matter.

What news had Timothy brought? It was terrific news and Paul was delighted. The Thessalonians were standing firm in their faith in Jesus. And more than that, they did have good memories of Paul's ministry in Thessalonica. These Christians were as keen to see Paul as he was to see them (v.6).

- ***So, good news. What do you notice about how this news affected Paul? How does Paul describe his reaction (vv.7–9)?***

'...now we really live,' Paul says (v.8). It is as if Paul had felt nearly dead, he feared for them so much. Timothy's news had brought Paul encouragement and joy in his own distress (v.7,9). And it had caused great thanksgiving to God to well up inside him. So great, in fact, that he could scarcely describe it (v.9).

Think of Christians you know who are standing firm in the Lord. Thank God for them and let their example encourage you.

- ***In the light of all this, why is verse 10 quite surprising?***

These Christians were doing well. So surely Paul could relax about them. Shouldn't he turn his attention to Christians somewhere else, to people who really were struggling? No.

Paul said he was praying day and night that he might be able to go and see the Thessalonians himself. He wanted to 'supply what [was] lacking in [their] faith'.

What was this all about? Paul loved these believers, and so of course he wanted to see them again. But it doesn't sound from the letter so far as if there *was* much lacking in their faith. They sound like a model church. In fact, Paul said that they are just that in 1:7.

So, why didn't Paul just turn his attention elsewhere? Why was he praying so earnestly and constantly for the chance to visit them again? After all, they were doing fine spiritually.

What we learn here is that all Christians need encouragement. Paul prayed for those who were going well in the faith as well as for those who were struggling. Everyone needs to have their faith built up all the time. Why? Because this side of heaven, our trust in Christ is constantly under attack. Pray for Christians you know who seem to be going well. Pray that they would keep growing in their faith in Jesus.

PRAY

- ***Thank God for the example of Christians you know who are 'standing firm' in Christ, even in the midst of trials.***
- ***Pray that you would be concerned about the spiritual health of other Christians.***
- ***Pray that you would want to keep growing in your faith in Christ.***
- ***Pray for Christians you know who seem to be going really well. Pray they would keep growing too.***

DAY 15

READ 1 Thessalonians 3:11–13

Do you ever wonder how you should pray for people? In today's verses, Paul lets us listen in to what he is praying for these new believers.

There are two prayers in this letter – one at the end of the first half, and one at the end of the second. The second prayer is in 5:23. Have a look at it.

- ***What do you notice about these two prayers?***

In both prayers Paul's big concern is what would happen on the day Jesus comes again as judge (3:13;5:23).

- ***What did Paul want for these Christians on that day (3:13)?***

Paul wanted these Christians to be 'blameless' on that day. What does 'blameless' mean? It doesn't mean that Paul was hoping that they would become totally sinless in this life. Sadly, all of us remain sinful this side of heaven. But it is possible not to be 'blamed' for our sin on the day we face Christ. If we continue to trust and serve Christ until the end of our lives then we will have nothing to fear on the day of judgement.

We will not be 'blamed' for our sin, because Jesus has taken that blame for us as He died on the cross. He has made us 'holy', that is, fit for God's presence. On that day, those who trust Christ will be forgiven and welcomed. And Paul prayed that that would happen to his friends. That was his goal for these Christians.

That was what Paul wanted for the Thessalonians in the future. So what did Paul pray for them now? Let's have a closer look at today's verses.

- ***What did Paul pray that he would be able to do (v.11)?***

- ***What did Paul pray that the Thessalonians would do (v.12)?***

- ***Whose example should they follow (v.12)?***

- ***How would God use these things in the lives of these believers (v.13)?***

Paul wanted to visit his friends (v.11). And he wanted them to love more and more. In particular, Paul wanted them to love in the same way that he had loved them (v.12).

What difference would it make if Paul did visit and if they did love each other more and more? It seems that these things were the means God would use to 'strengthen' their hearts (v.13). This was how God would help them keep going as Christians so that they would be 'blameless' on the day Jesus returns.

Paul had already sent Timothy to 'strengthen' them in their faith (3:2) and now Paul wanted to do the same for them himself. Paul prayed that God would help him get to see these believers. As you pray for Christians, pray that God would send people into their lives who would strengthen their faith in Christ. Pray that they wouldn't give up but would be blameless on the day Jesus comes.

What about this growing love that Paul prayed for? What was that about? In this letter Paul has been describing the love he himself had for these believers. We have read a great deal about this love in this first part of Paul's letter. Paul wanted these Christians to love each other in the same way, and to love everyone in this way too (v.12).

Do you remember how Paul had showed his love for these Christians? First, Paul had loved them by telling them about Jesus, even though this had not been easy (2:2). Now Paul wanted them to love outsiders in this way too. He wanted them to take the trouble to share the gospel, whatever the cost.

Secondly, Paul had loved these Thessalonians by helping them grow in their faith in Christ. Paul really cared about them. He had been like a mother (2:7,8) and like a father (2:11,12) in the way he had cared for them. Now Paul wanted his friends to love each other like that as well.

- ***What has all that got to do with God 'strengthen[ing their] hearts so that [they] will be blameless and holy' at the coming of Jesus (3:13)?***

Well, if Christians love each other like that then they too will strengthen each other's faith in Christ. They will help each other to be blameless on the day Jesus comes. God uses people in our lives to help us keep going as Christians. Pray that you would love other Christians in that way. And pray that you would love unbelievers enough to share Christ with them too.

PRAY

- ***Thank God that we can be 'blameless' on judgement day because of Jesus.***
- ***Ask God to strengthen your heart to keep trusting Jesus.***
- ***Ask God to help you love your fellow Christians more and more.***
- ***Ask God to help you model the way you love on the way Paul and Silas loved these Thessalonians.***
- ***Ask God to help you love people in a way which will strengthen their hearts to keep on trusting Christ until the end.***
- ***Thank God for the people He has sent into your life to love you and strengthen your faith in Jesus.***

DAY 16

READ 1 Thessalonians 4:1–3a

Today we are going to think about what God does and what we do in the Christian life. It is an important topic to think through and be clear on.

In the previous few verses we saw that Paul asked God to make these Christians 'blameless and holy'. We focused on what it means to be 'blameless'. We can be 'blameless' only by being forgiven through trusting Christ.

Today we are going to think some more about holiness. What exactly does holiness mean? To be holy means to be like God. We are to be pure and morally perfect. To be holy also means specially belonging to God. We are set apart for Him. In one sense we become holy the moment we become a Christian. By His grace, God sets us apart to belong to Him.

Now God calls us to make every effort to 'be what we are'. Our lives and our characters are to change for the better. We belong to God. God wants us to look more and more like Himself. In this sense we are to grow in holiness. Our trust in Christ is to be expressed in a growing holiness of life and character.

- ***What was God's will for these new believers (4:3)?***

God wanted them to grow in holiness. 'Sanctification' means becoming holy.

How does sanctification happen? Twice in this letter Paul prays for his friends. In both prayers, Paul is concerned that these believers should be holy. Have a look again at 3:11–13 and 5:23. So, who makes us holy? Who sanctifies us (5:23)? It is something that *God* does.

When you see a Christian's life and character changing for the better, you are seeing a work of God. Thank Him for it. And we need to keep asking God to be at work in us too. We need to ask Him to change our hearts and our lives more and more.

But does that mean that we just lie back and do nothing? Do we just wait for God to make us more and more like Himself – more holy? No.

- ***What does Paul ask and urge them to do in verses 1 to 2?***

Here, and through much of the second part of this letter, Paul urges these Christians to do things. They are to make every effort to live to please God (v.1).

God does make us more holy. But God does not do this by bypassing our personalities. We ourselves are to make every effort to listen to and obey God's Word. This is how we please Him. And God, by His Holy Spirit, gives us the strength to do that. Listening to God's

Word and obeying it is the means God uses to make us holy.

Let's pray that we would make every effort to listen to and obey God. When we do that we'll experience God's great power working in us. That is how God transforms us.

- ***Do we have to guess how to live to please God? What does Paul say in verses 1 to 2?***

It is clear that Paul had already given them 'instructions... by the authority of the Lord Jesus' (v.2) which they were already following (v.1).

It is very difficult to please someone if they don't tell you what pleases them. But these believers did know what would please Jesus. Paul is saying here that he had passed on to them what Jesus Himself wanted them to know. They did not have to play guessing games. They could know for certain what pleased God.

As we have seen before, Paul was one of Jesus' apostles (2:6). Jesus' apostles taught with Jesus' own authority. We can find these teachings in our New Testaments. So we need to be studying our Bibles very carefully. Then we too can know how to live to please God.

It seems these Christians in Thessalonica were already following Paul's instructions. Why did Paul urge them 'to do this more and more'? Whatever these believers were doing right in the Christian life, Paul wanted them to do that 'more and more'. We see that over and over again in this letter.

Being a Christian is a bit like staying on a bicycle. You need to keep going forward all the time. You need to keep making progress. Pray you would listen carefully to God's words in the Bible telling you how to please Him. And pray that you would follow God's instructions 'more and more'.

PRAY

- ***Thank God that He has set you apart to belong to Him, to be holy.***
- ***Thank God for what He has already done in you to change you.***
- ***Ask God to help you to 'be what you are', to live a holy life.***
- ***Thank God that He has spoken to you clearly in the Bible and told you how to live to please Him.***
- ***Ask God to help you make every effort to listen to and to obey His Word more and more.***

DAY 17

READ 1 Thessalonians 4:3–8

What do you want most in life? What would you say if you were asked that question?

- ***What is your biggest hope for your life?***

God's big plan for your life is that you become holy. God wants you to become the person He made you to be. You were made to reflect the character of God Himself.

Paul has been reminding these new believers of God's will for their lives. God wanted them to be sanctified – that is, to be made holy (v.3). So Paul has been urging his friends to follow his instructions about how to please God. And he wanted them to do so 'more and more'.

Now Paul reminds them of three specific ways they needed to live to please God:

1. Holiness in sexual behaviour.
2. Love for all fellow Christians.
3. Daily lives which make Christ attractive to those who are not yet Christian.

Today we look at sexual behaviour.

The background to what Paul says here is the Bible's clear and consistent teaching about sex. God designed sexual union to be an expression of the union of a man and a woman in lifelong marriage. Sex both expresses and seals the marriage promise to give yourself wholly and uniquely to your spouse 'till death us do part'. To have sex in any context outside heterosexual marriage is to break God's law. It is a sin against God. It is also to 'wrong' the other person involved (v.6).

- ***Let's look closely at what Paul teaches here. What did God want them to do (v.3)?***

The word Paul uses for sexual immorality means all sexual activity outside heterosexual marriage. Sexual desires are very powerful. Our society often treats sexual desire as just a bodily appetite. It is seen as an appetite that we should 'feed' whenever we feel 'hungry'.

- ***But Paul says that Christians are to be different. Rather than being controlled by their bodily urges, what should the Christian do (v.4)?***

Christians are to abstain from all sexual immorality. They are to learn to control their own bodies (v.4).

- ***How does Paul describe what a Christian should do with his or her body (vv.4–6)?***

What a Christian does with his/her body should be 'holy and honourable' (v.4). It should not be driven by lust (v.5). It should not be sinful (v.6). To behave in a way which breaks God's law wrongs God. But it also wrongs the other person involved (v.6). We need to pray that we would learn to control our bodies so that we only use them in holy and honourable ways.

- ***How do you react to Paul's words here?***

Many of us will probably feel failures in this area. We need to repent and come to God again for His forgiveness. It is good to remember that there is no sin which cannot be forgiven by God. Jesus died so that every, every, every sin could be forgiven.

God's Word often uncovers our sin. This can make us feel uncomfortable and exposed. But God can use this experience for great good in our lives. When we see sin for what it is, it can help us turn from that sin decisively. It can also help us cling closely to Christ. For when we see our sin clearly, we see our need for salvation clearly too. We need to confront our own sin and turn from it. But we also need to rejoice in the certainty of God's forgiveness.

Maybe we feel that learning 'to control [our bodies] in a way that is holy and honourable' is going to be quite beyond us. Paul gives us serious warnings here. But he also gives us encouragements as we face this challenge. These warnings and encouragements will help us learn to be holy in our sexual behaviour. We need to heed them carefully.

First, the warnings.

- ***What does Paul tell these believers about God in verse 6?***

God takes sin very seriously. God sees all sin. He sees even the sin which we hide from other people. There is no such thing as 'private' sin or sin 'behind closed doors'. God sees it all. And He will take action to judge it. Paul says he had 'warned' them about this matter before.

- ***What does Paul remind them of in verse 8?***

God has made his views about sex abundantly clear in His Word. Paul reminds these Christians that what he is teaching is from God Himself. The Christian person knows and loves God. Sexual immorality wrongs both God and the other person involved.

Look at verse 6 again. If you really know and love God, there is no way you can go on behaving like this. Those who do not know God will do exactly what they like. You can see their behaviour described in verse 5. The Christian is to be different.

- ***Then secondly, there are great encouragements here. What has God called us to (v.7)?***

- ***What has God given us (v.8)?***

We are not on our own in this struggle to be holy. God has given us His Holy Spirit. God's Spirit lives in us and strengthens us in the fight to be holy.

God Himself has also called us to be holy. God has saved us not just *from* wrath (1:10), but also *for* holiness (v.7). God wants us to be the people He made us to be.

PRAY

- ***Thank God that because of Jesus, He forgives every sin and failure in your life.***
- ***Thank God that He has called you to a new way of living, in holiness and purity.***
- ***Thank God for the gift of His Holy Spirit to help you change and live differently.***
- ***Ask God to help you remember that the Bible's teachings about sexual behaviour are words that come from God.***
- ***Ask God to help you to abstain from all sexual immorality and to learn to control your body in a way that is holy and honourable.***
- ***Ask God to help you take the warnings in today's passage seriously.***

DAY 18

READ 1 Thessalonians 4:9,10

'...do this more and more ...we urge you, brothers, to do so more and more'.

Did you spot that little phrase again? It seems that wherever Paul saw these believers doing something well, he commended them. And then he urged them to do that good thing, whatever it was, more and more. He wanted them to keep growing all the time. For that is the way to stay safe as a Christian. Even strong points in our Christian lives can quickly turn into weak ones if we start taking them for granted. So, whatever is going well, do it more and more.

- ***What was it that these Thessalonian Christians were doing so well (v.9)?***

- ***What is Paul talking about here?***

Let your eyes skim over the text of the whole letter. You will see that Paul uses the term 'brothers' over and over again. It was his favourite way of referring to Christians. To become a Christian is to be adopted into God's own family. We come to know God as our loving heavenly Father. We also find that every other believer in Christ is a close family member, a 'brother'.

Paul does not use the word 'brother' because everyone in the church was around his age and male. The word 'brother' shows us the closeness of relationship which all Christians share. Fellow Christians are not distant cousins twice removed. We are close relatives. We are committed to each other. We are family.

The word 'brother' also shows us that we are all equal. Other Christians are neither our lords nor our slaves. Even church leaders such as Paul or Timothy (3:2) remain our 'brothers' in Christ. So, in speaking of 'brotherly love' here, Paul was speaking of the sort of close, committed, affectionate family love which brothers should share. Perhaps you have already begun to experience this? Christians share a unique love for one another within the family of God. It is one of the great delights of being part of a church family. We pray, learn and share with other Christians, and find that there is a special bond and love between us. Thank God for the love which other Christians have shown you.

Paul says two things here about the love these believers have for each other:

- ***First, who did they love? Look at verse 10.***

This was not just love for one or two special Christian friends. These Christians were showing brotherly love to 'all the brothers throughout Macedonia' (that's the whole region around their city).

Pray that your church would be marked by brotherly love for all those in the fellowship. Pray that you would be concerned for Christians in other parts of the country and the world as well.

- ***Secondly, how did these Christians come to love like this (v.9)?***

This was something that God Himself had 'taught' them to do.

What does this mean? It means that God Himself had shown them how to love. God had given them a model to follow. God had shown them His own costly love in giving up His only Son for them.

God had also put His love into their hearts. God had given them a supernatural bond with other believers within the Christian family. Other Christians share the same Spirit, the same Saviour, and the same heavenly Father. Paul wanted his friends to develop this love, but they had not had to create it. God had already done that.

Pray that you would love other Christians like this, and do so more and more. How could you show love and care to others in your church more than you do?

PRAY

- ***Thank God for loving you so much that He sent Jesus to die for you.***
- ***Thank God for showing you how to love.***
- ***Thank God for putting love for other Christians into your heart by His Spirit.***
- ***Ask God to help you show love and care to all in your church family, and to do that more and more.***
- ***Ask God to help you find out more about Christians in other places so that you can pray for them and help them too.***

DAY 19

READ 1 Thessalonians 4:11,12

Did you know a Christian before you became a believer yourself?

Often it is the example and witness of a friend or family member which first begins to point someone to Jesus. Maybe that was your experience.

Sadly, the reverse is also true. When people are asked why they are not Christians, many point to bad experiences of people who say they are Christians.

The Thessalonian believers clearly had a great reputation among their fellow Christians (1:7;4:10). But Paul wanted them to be a good advertisement for Jesus among unbelievers also.

- ***What did Paul want them to do (v.12)?***

What is Paul talking about here? Sometimes people talk about 'the watching world'. And it is true that, wherever we are, people do take note of how we live. They watch. They notice. Paul was concerned that his friends' daily lives should be attractive and good. It is no good speaking for Jesus with our mouths if our lives speak against Him. How we live can put people off becoming Christians. What does the way you live say about Jesus?

- ***So, how should these believers live? What should be their ambition (v.11)?***

It all sounds rather mundane and ordinary, doesn't it? They were to lead 'quiet lives'. This doesn't mean that they were to talk in whispers. It means that their lives should be free of the 'noise' of scandal.

They were to 'mind [their] own business'. This doesn't mean that they were to live like islands. Of course Christians are to look for opportunities to help those who are in need. But believers should not be gossips and busybodies. They should not have a nose in everyone else's business. They should not go sniffing for juicy titbits of gossip or interfering in the private affairs of other people.

What is this about working 'with your hands, just as we told you... so that you will not be dependent on anybody'? Do we all have to do manual work?

The key point here seems to be that Christians were to work, in whatever way they could. Maybe some in Thessalonica thought manual work was below them. But Paul did manual work. He sewed tents at night in order to finance his day job as a gospel preacher. Paul had taught them that manual work was honourable.

Why were Christians to work, if they were able to do so? So that they could be givers rather than takers.

- ***What does Paul say about this at the end of verse 12?***

Paul did not want these Christians to be constantly scrounging off their non-Christian neighbours. Such behaviour would give the believers a bad name. It would not speak of the grace and generosity of God in the gospel. In many, many ways, the way we live ordinary life speaks volumes about us and about Christ.

Think about your own daily life. What could you change to make it a better advert for Christ and His gospel?

PRAY

- ***Pray that your daily life would speak of God's holiness, His love and His generous grace.***
- ***Pray that your life would be free from scandal, gossiping and laziness.***
- ***Pray that you would do your daily work well and live a life full of generosity to those around you.***
- ***Pray that in every way your life would be a good advert for Christ and His gospel.***
- ***Ask God to help you see what you need to change, and to help you to do that.***

DAY 20

READ 1 Thessalonians 4:13,14

What we believe about the future has a big effect on how we live in the present.

Ask any student in the summer term. If we know exams are coming, we get down to revision *now*. Or we should do.

There is much about the future we don't know. But one thing we do know for sure. Jesus is coming. He is coming as the Judge of all people and the Saviour of those who trust and follow Him. Do you remember 1:10? Jesus is coming and He will save us from 'the coming wrath'. This final event of history coloured how Paul saw everything in the present. It motivated him to keep going and growing in the Christian life. It motivated him to encourage others to keep going too. Our readings over the next few days focus on Christ's return. Let's pray it motivates us just as it did Paul.

Maybe you haven't thought much about Jesus coming back. Jesus is no longer physically present on earth, but He promised He will return one day in great glory. Paul talks about what will happen (4:13–18) and also about how it should affect us now (5:1–11).

Have a look at the verses which close these two sections, 4:18 and 5:11.

- ***What did Paul want them to do with this teaching about Jesus' return?***

We are to encourage one another by reminding each other that Jesus is coming back. We will suffer now for being Christians, but it will be worth it. Our future with Jesus is assured.

It seems that some of the believers in Thessalonica had already died ('fall[en] asleep', as Paul puts it in v.13). Perhaps those still living were wondering if something had gone wrong. Jesus had conquered death, hadn't He? Why were Christians dying like everybody else, then? And would these dead Christians miss out on being reunited with Christ when He did come back?

- ***What did Paul want for them (v.13a)?***

Paul did not want these believers to be in the dark about what was going to happen. He was very keen for them to know the truth about their Christian friends who had already died. Many people speculate about what happens after death. But Jesus Christ is the only reliable expert on this subject. It is vital we know the truth about this because all of us will die. This is not just an academic question. Jesus is the only person who has risen from death, never to die again. So, it is very reassuring indeed to have the words of Jesus' apostle here. Paul can tell us the truth on this important subject.

- ***What will God do for Christians who die before Jesus comes back (v.14)?***

Paul's big point is that we can be certain that Christians who die will be raised to be with Christ.

- ***How could his friends be sure this would happen? What does Paul say about this in verse 14?***

We have this certain hope because of Jesus' resurrection. If we are joined to Jesus Christ by faith, then we will share His resurrection 'with' Him. A needle and thread are joined together. Wherever the needle goes the thread will follow. So it is with Christ and us. God took Christ through death to resurrection and new life. And where Christ has gone, we will follow. We are joined to Christ by faith. God's mighty power raised Christ. God can raise us too.

Paul spoke of Christians who had died as being 'asleep'. He meant that for them death was only a temporary state. It was nothing to be scared of. People who are asleep wake up to a new day. Believers too will 'wake' from death to new life with Christ in His new creation.

- ***So, how should Christians respond when their fellow believers die (v.13)?***

Christians do grieve when fellow believers die. Even temporary separation is very, very painful. But Christian grief is different. It is different because we know resurrection and reunion are coming. Thank God that we can know for certain that those who die trusting Christ will be raised to new life.

PRAY

- ***Thank God that He raised Jesus to new life, and that He will raise us also.***
- ***Thank God that He has shown us the truth about what happens after death.***
- ***Thank God that for those trusting Christ, death is no scarier than going to sleep.***
- ***Ask God to comfort those you know who grieve the loss of Christian friends or family. Pray that they would know hope in the midst of their grief.***

DAY 21

READ 1 Thessalonians 4:15–18

Christians who die before Jesus' return will be raised to be with Christ. That is absolutely certain. Now Paul goes on to explain how this will happen.

- ***Remember, we are looking for encouragements (v.18). What do you find encouraging as you read these verses?***

First, notice again that this is not speculation. Look at verse 15. What Paul describes here is certain to happen. We can be certain about it because Paul is passing on Jesus' own words. This is what Jesus wants us to know about his coming.

Secondly, we see God's authority here. As we read this description, we see a picture which is full of God's power and authority. Look at verse 16. It is full of details which speak of God's authority. The 'loud command', the 'voice of the archangel' and 'the trumpet call of God'. These are all sounds which communicate God's supreme authority over everything. What God says happens.

We see God's great power in action too. God raised Jesus. Jesus is not dead. He is 'the Lord'. He is in 'heaven' now and He will come to us from that place of authority. All the 'dead in Christ', those who have died trusting Christ, 'will rise first'. God raised Jesus' corpse from the dead by His mighty power. And He will do the same for yours. God is all-powerful.

Thank God that He has promised to raise you with Christ.

So, certainty, authority, and then the third big truth in these verses is reunion.

These Thessalonian Christians were missing their dead friends. Death is a separation which hurts so much. Would they ever see these Christian friends again? When they died, these Christians were loving Jesus. They were eagerly waiting for His return. Would they ever get to see Jesus? Or had they missed out?

- ***What did Paul say about these questions in verse 17?***

Had these Christians missed out? Paul's answer is a resounding 'No!' Paul has much good news for his anxious friends. Look at verse 17. Christians who are still alive when Jesus returns 'will be caught up together with them' (that is, with Christians who have already died). So, they will be reunited. They will be 'together with them' again.

This reunion of Christians will be just part of the big purpose of that great day. For who else will we meet on that day? The Lord Jesus Himself. What a wonderful prospect that is. We will see

Jesus face to face: Jesus, who loved us and gave His life to save us.

And the last phrase of verse 17 is the most wonderful of all: 'And so we will be with the Lord for ever.'

This meeting with Jesus isn't going to be a brief handshake with a VIP who we will then never see again. God wants to live with us. God's purpose in sending Jesus to die for us was to bring us back to a restored relationship with Himself. God's heart's desire is for us to live with Him, as forgiven people. We will be together with Him, and with each other, forever.

We don't see Jesus now. And we don't see our Christian friends who have died. But one day we will. Separation will be over. It will be over forever. Thank God for these great truths about your future.

PRAY

- ***Thank God that His Word is trustworthy and true.***
- ***Thank God that He is in control of the future.***
- ***Thank God that on the last day His power and glory will be clearly seen.***
- ***Thank God that we will be reunited with Christians who have died.***
- ***Thank God that we will meet Jesus on the last day and live with Him always.***
- ***Pray that you would have an opportunity to encourage other Christians with these great truths.***

READ 1 Thessalonians 5:1–3

'If I had known you were coming today I would have got ready.'

It can be so helpful to know when visitors are going to arrive, or when workmen are coming to do a job in our home. Then we can tidy up. Or we can move the furniture out of the room that's having the new carpet or whatever. But sometimes people arrive unexpectedly and we're just not ready for them.

Do we know when Jesus is coming? Paul has just been telling these believers about what will happen on that great day. Now Paul turns his attention to the timing, 'times and dates' (v.1). When will all this happen? After all, we do want to be ready for Jesus when He comes.

Paul uses two pictures to remind these Christians of what they clearly already knew (v.1). He says that the timing of Jesus' coming ('the day of the Lord') will be like the arrival of a burglar in the night, and like the arrival of labour pains to a woman about to give birth.

- ***What do these pictures – the thief and the labour pains – tell us about Jesus' return?***

You never know when a burglar may break into your house. He doesn't send you a postcard to tell you when he is coming. If he did, you would be wide awake and ready to stop him. Jesus is clearly not a burglar. But we don't know when He will come, either. We just don't know when it will be, any more than we know which night we will be burgled. Many people will be taken completely by surprise by Jesus' return. Unbelievers won't be expecting it at all.

- ***What will people be saying on the day Jesus comes back (v.3)?***

They will begin the day feeling secure, with no inkling of what is coming.

- ***And what is coming, for those who are not trusting and following Christ? What does verse 3 tell us?***

Jesus is coming as Judge of all people. The day Jesus returns as Judge will be a day of disaster for some. It will be a terrible day for those who have not turned away from idols and turned to Christ for forgiveness – 'destruction will come on them suddenly... and they will not escape' (v.3).

It will be too late to change your mind about Jesus on that day – there will be no 'escape' then. Pray for unbelievers you know to turn to Christ whilst they still have time.

- ***What about the picture of labour pains? What is the point of this picture?***

When women go to their antenatal classes they are told a lot about being in labour. But one thing they are never told is exactly when their own labour pains will begin. Because no one knows.

Like the thief in the night, labour pains arrive 'suddenly' (v.3). But unlike the thief in the night, labour pains should not be a surprise. A heavily pregnant woman knows that labour pains will definitely arrive. She just doesn't know exactly when.

In verse 4, Paul says that for Christians, Jesus' coming should not be a 'surprise' either, even though it will be sudden. We don't know when it will happen. But we do know that it is coming. So we should be ready, ready all the time.

Paul is going to explain what it means to be ready in the following verses. Pray we would be ready for Jesus on the day He returns. Pray that we would be living in a way which pleases Him. It could be today.

PRAY

- ***Pray for unbelievers you know to become Christians before Christ returns.***
- ***Pray that you would live to please Jesus every single day, so that you will be ready for Him when He comes, whenever that is.***

DAY 23

READ 1 Thessalonians 5:4–8

'I'm totally in the dark about...'

'In the dark' is an expression we use to mean we just don't 'see' or understand something.

Paul has been reminding these believers that they should not be 'in the dark' about the return of Jesus Christ. That day may well be a total surprise to non-believers. For them it will be as surprising as finding a burglar in your home. But Jesus' return should not be a surprise to Christians. We should be ready for Jesus at all times. We are not 'in the dark'. We know He is coming.

Paul uses this idea of darkness versus light to help his friends think more deeply about how to be ready for Jesus.

- ***What ideas does Paul associate with darkness?***

- ***What ideas does he associate with light?***

Paul pictures unbelievers as being people who 'belong to the night'. He associates night-time with darkness, with being asleep and with drunkenness.

Paul's point is that unbelievers are not in touch with reality. Like someone asleep, they don't even know they are in danger. Like someone blind drunk near the edge of a cliff in pitch darkness, they don't know how to keep safe.

When you are asleep or drunk, you don't know what is happening around you. You are 'out of it'. And if you are in total darkness you don't know where you are, either.

Asleep. Drunk. In the dark. Don't live like that, Paul says, because you, Christians, 'belong to the day' (v.8).

- ***'You are all sons of the light and sons of the day' (v.5). What does that mean?***

Daytime is associated with light, with being awake, with being sober. Paul is using picture language here. He didn't mean that Christians should never go out after dark or never go to sleep physically.

His point is that these Christians were wide awake to the fact that Christ was coming. They were in touch with reality. And so they, and we, should live each day in the light of this certain future.

Paul says, stay awake and stay sober. Don't nod off. Don't lose control of yourselves. Don't forget that Jesus is coming, and that it could be at any time.

- ***What will 'belong[ing] to the day' look like in practice (v.8)?***

Paul wanted them to stay 'alert and self-controlled'. He wanted them to be sober. Paul wanted them to keep their 'armour' strapped on. Paul talks here about their faith, love and hope of salvation as being different pieces of armour. Why do you think he used those images?

Being a Christian is not a picnic. It is like being in a war. We have enemies against us. The devil tempts us. People around us may oppose us and want us to stop being Christians. We still have a sinful nature which loves to be selfish. There is real spiritual danger and we need protection.

How will we keep safe in the battle against all these enemies? God has given us armour to protect us. We need to keep our armour on. That is, we need to keep on trusting and loving Jesus. We need to keep hoping for Jesus' return. Paul talks as if Christians are soldiers who are on duty all the time. We need to be on 'red alert' spiritually every day. Because Jesus is coming.

PRAY

- ***Thank God that He has brought you out of spiritual darkness into His wonderful light.***
- ***Ask Him to help you to remember every day that Jesus is coming.***
- ***Pray you would keep trusting, loving and hoping in Jesus, so that you are ready to meet Him when He comes.***

READ 1 Thessalonians 5:9–11

Do you ever worry that you won't stay a Christian?

It is easy to focus on all the dangers and difficulties which face us as Christians and to be discouraged. How will we ever make it?

Paul has just been talking about putting on battle armour, and the need to stay awake. He wanted his friends to be alert and self-controlled so that they would be ready for Christ when He comes.

It all sounds like a lot of hard work. So, is it all up to us, then? Does our spiritual safety depend on us? There would not be much hope for us if it did. We are so weak and sinful.

In verses 9 and 10 Paul puts the spotlight back on what God had done to save these believers. If they were Christians, they had put on the spiritual armour of faith, love and hope in Christ (v.8). That is true. And they did need to keep it on. But how was it that they had come to have this faith, love and hope in Christ?

- ***What is Paul's answer in verse 9? What had God done for these Christians?***

God had already chosen their final destination. Paul was sure that these Christians would experience God's salvation on the last day and not His wrath against their sin.

That is very encouraging. But how did Paul know? How could he be so sure?

Have a look back to chapter 1 verses 2 to 10. Here Paul describes the Christian faith of his friends in Thessalonica. Now focus in particular on verses 4 and 5. Paul says here that he knew that God had chosen these Thessalonian believers. He knew this because of the way they had responded to the gospel message and the way that they had begun to live differently. They were following Jesus, despite the suffering it had brought them.

And all this was not a result of them being more intelligent or better than other people. It was all the work of God's Spirit (1:5,6).

So, these Thessalonian believers had become people who had faith, love and hope in Jesus. Just as Paul had. They had put on that 'breastplate' and 'helmet' (5:8). That was a mark of God being at work in them. Paul was sure that God would finish what He had started. He would save them on the last day.

Thank God that He will finish what He has chosen to begin in your life.

Paul reminded his friends that God would save them on the last day. But he also reminded them of how God had accomplished that salvation, and why. These things too were to encourage them to keep going as Christians.

- ***How had God saved them? (Look at the end of v.9 and the beginning of v.10.)***

God's just punishment for sin is death. Jesus has already taken this punishment 'for us'. He 'died for us', in our place. So now we, who trust Him, will never have to experience the rightful anger of God against our sin. The only way 'to receive salvation' is 'through' Him (v.9), through Jesus and His death for us. Thank Jesus for dying for you.

- ***And why did our Lord Jesus Christ willingly die for us to save us from the anger and punishment of God that we deserve?***
- ***What is the answer Paul gives in verse 10?***

Jesus did not die for us so we could just file away a forgiveness certificate in our bottom drawer and carry on ignoring God. Jesus' aim in dying for us was to bring us into a new loving relationship with Himself.

Yes, we need forgiveness to bring us into that new relationship. But His purpose in forgiving us is that we might 'live... with him', both now and in the new creation He is bringing. One day we will see Jesus face to face. And we will live with Him forever. It is a wonderful prospect.

It won't matter whether we are alive or dead physically ('awake or asleep', v.10) when Jesus comes back. Either way, we will be with Him forever. That is certain. Thank God for His desire to live with you.

God saves us. Our confidence for the future lies in Him, not in our own efforts.

Paul has been urging these Christians to make every effort to keep going, to stay self-controlled and alert spiritually. But their efforts did not win or earn their salvation.

They were to make an effort *because* God had already decided to save them. Jesus had died for them. God had destined them for salvation. God wanted to live with them forever.

So, Paul is saying, don't give up! Keep going until Jesus comes! And keep encouraging and building each other up so that all of you make it. Pray for opportunities to use these truths to help another Christian keep going too.

PRAY

- ***Thank God for appointing you for salvation through faith in Jesus.***
- ***Thank Jesus for dying for you.***
- ***Thank Him too for His plan and desire to live with you always.***
- ***Pray you would encourage others in their faith in Christ too.***

Jesus is coming.

Paul has been specifically talking about that great fact since chapter 4 verse 13. And it has been clearly on his mind all the way through this letter.

Have a look back to Paul's prayer for these Christians at the end of chapter 3.

Jesus is coming (3:14). Paul wanted his friends to live lives which would be pleasing to Jesus. So he prayed for them to become increasingly holy.

(Remember, Paul did not see growing in holiness as a means of earning salvation, but as a way of showing the genuineness of the salvation they had already received.)

Then all the way through chapters 4 and 5 Paul has been telling these believers how to live holy lives. They needed to follow Paul's instructions if they wanted to please God (4:1–3a).

Here at the end of chapter 5, Paul gives these believers some practical and specific instructions. He tells them about ways he wanted them to grow in holiness as they waited for Jesus' return.

In today's verses, Paul tells them what attitude they should have towards their church leaders. He calls their leaders 'those... who are over you in the Lord' (v.12).

- ***What does Paul say about what these leaders were doing in the church family?***

Some people see having authority as the chance to tell others to do all the work, while the person in authority sits back and puts his or her feet up.

Having authority in the church is never like that. Twice Paul draws attention to the hard work of those who were leading the church. Leading a church family was, and is, very hard work.

What exactly do church leaders do? Paul mentions just one of their responsibilities here. He says they 'admonish'. Admonish means to correct someone who is in the wrong, and to call them back to do what is right. Everyone in the church has a responsibility to do this, but it is a particular responsibility of the church leader, and it is probably one of the hardest things church leaders have to do.

Telling Christians when they are going off track and calling on them to change can be extremely painful and difficult. But it is a vital way of serving the Christian family and keeping them safe.

Why does Paul mention it here? Maybe because it's easy to have a bad attitude to our leaders when they admonish us. We don't like people telling us we are wrong and that we need to change. It's easy to want to hit back. It's easy to start being rebellious against those who are 'over [us] in the Lord' (v.12). But Paul wanted these Christians to 'Live in peace with each other' (v.13). So they needed to have the right attitude to their leaders.

- ***What attitude should these believers have to their church leaders who were working so hard?***

God cares about our attitudes as well as our actions.

In fact, our actions flow out of our attitudes. Paul says these believers should respect and love their leaders. They should esteem them very highly.

Notice that Paul links his friends' attitude to these leaders to how the leaders were behaving. The believers were to 'Hold them in the highest regard in love because of their work' (v.13). They should 'respect those who work hard among you' (v.12).

Elsewhere in the New Testament there are many warnings about the dangers of false teachers taking leadership in the church.

The leaders who deserve our respect are those who work hard at teaching God's Word. Good leaders lead and care for their congregations by teaching the Bible. They do not shy away from admonishing those who are going wrong.

Those who lead in the church are of equal status with those they lead. All Christians are 'brothers', having equal status before God. But 'in the Lord' some are given a role of being 'over' the congregation, in order to lead and care for them. We need to honour and respect their leadership.

PRAY

- ***Thank God for the work of those who lead your church.***
- ***Ask God to help them teach His Word faithfully, and admonish those who do wrong.***
- ***Ask God to help you respect and love your church leaders for their good work.***

What were your expectations of belonging to a church family?

Hopefully you have been warmly welcomed at the church you have joined. Hopefully you have begun to learn and to serve others.

It can be a bit of a shock, though, to discover that belonging to a church has its tensions as well as its joys – although we should not really be surprised, because a church is a gathering of sinful people. Yes, we are forgiven. Yes, we have been given the gift of the Holy Spirit to begin to change us. But we remain sinful and needy. And so living together in the church will have its difficulties and demands.

In today's verses, Paul tells his readers how to behave when being in a church family is challenging.

- ***What difficulties or needs can you find in these verses?***

It seems that Paul knew very well that at times Christians will wrong each other. They will be tempted to get back at those who hurt them. At times they will be exasperating, weak, lazy, down-hearted, selfish and just plain contrary.

So when you find people in your church like that, don't be surprised. They may be feeling the same about you!

- ***Who was to take action to help in these needy and difficult situations?***

It is very tempting to see it as the church leaders' job to sort out any difficulties and needs in the church family. And it is true; they do have an overall responsibility to make sure that those things get done. But Paul clearly saw it as *everyone's* job.

So, Paul urged 'you, brothers...' to do all these things.

- ***What is the right response to idleness?***

- ***To timidity?***

- ***To weakness?***

- ***To being wronged?***

- ***What does Paul say about the general way these Christians should treat each other?***

- ***Can you see how each response would be appropriate and helpful to each person?***

- ***Can you see how Paul's general instructions tell us how we should approach individual relationships?***

All relationships are to be marked by patience. The weak might need help again and again. The idle might need to be gently challenged more than once. These Christians were to actively pursue peace. This might mean apologising! They were to actively look for ways to do good to each other, and to those outside the church.

It is an attractive picture – not of a perfect community, but of a community which reflects the forgiveness, grace, love and Lordship of Jesus.

PRAY

- ***Pray that your own church family would reflect the forgiveness, grace, love and Lordship of Jesus.***
- ***Pray you would put into practice what Paul teaches here.***
- ***Pray for wisdom to know what each individual needs, and how to help them.***
- ***Pray that you would accept help from others when you are in need yourself.***

READ 1 Thessalonians 5:16–18

Relationships. Paul has been telling these Christians how to relate to their leaders. He has been telling them how to relate to individuals in their church fellowship. Now he turns to their relationship with God.

- ***Paul tells his friends to do three things here. What are they?***

- ***What do you notice about how they were to do each of them?***

- ***What does Paul say about why they should do these things (v.18)?***

Is Paul being a bit unrealistic here? Would he have done better to write, 'Be joyful when things are going well. Pray at bedtime. Give thanks when you are in good circumstances'?

But Paul didn't say that. Instead he told his Christian friends to be 'joyful always', to 'pray continually', to 'give thanks in all circumstances'.

Didn't Paul realise that all of us have sad days, busy days and days when awful things happen?

The key to understanding what Paul meant here is in that little phrase 'in Christ Jesus'. To become a Christian is to be united to Jesus. By faith we are united to Jesus in His death and resurrection. Through His death our sins are fully and finally paid for. This means we will never face God's wrath against our sin. In Jesus' resurrection we see that Jesus is Lord. We see what will happen to us in the future. We will be raised to live with Jesus forever. He chose us. He loved us. We belong to Him, now and forever.

Those are truths which the ups and downs of life do not change. Whatever happens to us today, we can thank God for Jesus.

Paul did not say that we should thank God *for* all circumstances. He said we should thank God *in* all circumstances. Even when terrible things happen to us we can still thank God for what Jesus has done for us in His death and resurrection. We can rejoice in the fact that we belong to Him.

Jesus has died to bring us to know God as our loving heavenly Father. So we will want to be speaking to our Father throughout our day. Sometimes we will just cry out 'help me' or 'thank you' inside our heads. Sometimes we will set aside longer times to talk to Him.

Having someone to pray with is a great help too. Why not ask a Christian friend if they will get together with you to pray?

God sent His Son so that we could enjoy knowing Him. That is what we were made for, a love relationship with Him. So, God wants us to be people whose lives are full of knowing Him – rejoicing in Him, praying to Him and thanking Him.

It is in knowing and loving God like this that we will receive His strength to love other people in the way Paul has just been describing (5:12–15).

PRAY

- ***Thank God for all Jesus has done for you.***
- ***Thank God that whatever else happens to you today, you are secure in His love.***
- ***Ask God to help you think about all the blessings He has given you through Jesus so that you would be 'joyful always'.***
- ***Ask God to help you keep praying to Him as you go through the day.***

DAY 28

READ 1 Thessalonians 5:19–22

'God... gives you his Holy Spirit.'

We read those wonderful words back in chapter 4 verse 8. When someone becomes a Christian, God Himself comes to live in that person. God the Holy Spirit makes His home in our hearts.

God's Spirit begins to change us, to make us more and more the people God wants us to be. God wants us to be holy people. He wants us to be people who love God, people who share God's priorities and God's character.

- ***How does the Holy Spirit do His work of changing us?***

He does it through God's Word, as we listen to it and respond obediently. As we noted before, in another letter Paul called the Word of God 'the sword of the Spirit' (Ephesians 6:17). That means God's Word is the instrument the Spirit uses to do His work in us.

Paul has mentioned the Holy Spirit three times before in our Thessalonian letter. And each time Paul linked the Holy Spirit's work to God's Word.

The Holy Spirit was at work in these Christians to enable them to receive the gospel word with conviction and joy (1:5,6).

In chapter 4, Paul called on these believers to treat his teachings as God's word (4:2,8) and he instructed them about how to live holy lives. And in chapter 4 verse 8 Paul said that his friends ought to have an obedient attitude to these teachings because of the presence of the Holy Spirit in their lives.

We have just read nearly two chapters of Paul's instructions about how to grow in holiness.

- ***What does Paul say now about the Holy Spirit (v.19)?***

Paul had nearly finished his letter. His readers had nearly read it all now. They had all these words from God through Paul fresh in their minds. These are words which the Holy Spirit could use to transform them and strengthen them. But this would only happen if they paid close attention to these words and responded to them obediently.

So, Paul says, 'Do not put out the Spirit's fire'. It is as if he is picturing the Holy Spirit as a holy fire, purging all evil from our lives. And Paul is saying here, don't put that fire out. Don't stop the Spirit doing His work in you.

The Holy Spirit can grow holiness in you if you respond rightly to God's words here in this letter.

Pray that you too would listen to these words carefully, take them to heart and put them into practice. Then you will not 'put out the Spirit's fire' either.

- ***Then Paul goes on to speak about prophecies. What instructions does he give about them?***

The Bible uses the term 'prophecies' in a number of different ways. Some parts of the Bible are called prophecies. In the Old Testament, we meet many people who are called prophets. Old Testament prophets were people who prophesied; that means they spoke words from God. Old Testament prophets, such as Isaiah and Jeremiah, were people who spoke with the absolute authority of God.

In the New Testament, helpful words which Christians said to one another are sometimes called 'prophecies' (1 Corinthians 14:3). These words were not authoritative in the same way that the Scriptures were. They needed to be tested or 'weighed' (1 Corinthians 14:29). Such words were to be tested against the Bible to see if they should be accepted or rejected.

Paul's instructions in verses 20 to 22 seem to be about how to treat things that other Christians say to us. Paul seems to be using 'prophecies' in that sense here. When someone in the church shares a thought, an insight or a conviction, what should we do? We should neither dismiss these words nor accept them uncritically. We should test them.

We need to cling tightly to whatever we find to be good. God can use such words to help us greatly. But we must have nothing to do with anything evil.

So, we must not be dismissive. But we must be discerning. Pray that God would help you to be both those things as you listen to things Christians say.

PRAY

- ***Thank God for the gift of His Spirit in your life.***
- ***Pray you would not 'quench' the Spirit's work of making you increasingly holy.***
- ***Pray that you would carefully obey God's words in the Bible.***
- ***Pray you would learn to test the words of other Christians against the Bible.***

READ 1 Thessalonians 5:23,24

Paul is about to say goodbye to his friends. How will they keep going in their Christian faith?

As he draws his letter to a close, once again Paul prays for these believers. He prays for them 'continually', just as he has urged them to do too (5:17). His friends were in constant need of God's help.

Paul prayed for his friends back in chapter 3 verses 11 to 13. Have a look over that prayer again. Now look at Paul's prayer in today's verses.

- ***What similarities can you find between these two prayers?***

All the way through his letter, Paul has had his eyes on the last day. The day when Jesus comes back has been on his mind all the time. That day will be a day of terrible judgement for those who reject Christ. But it will be a day of wonderful salvation for those who trust and serve Him.

Above everything else, Paul wanted his Thessalonian friends to make it to this last day as Christians. He wanted them to keep trusting and serving Christ right up to the end. He wanted them to keep growing in holiness.

Growth in holiness is the evidence that a person's repentance and trust in Christ is genuine. On the last day, such a person will be found to be 'blameless'. That is, they will not be 'blamed' for any of their sins. Instead they will be totally forgiven through Jesus' death in their place.

- ***What did Paul ask God to do for his friends in verses 23 and 24? (Remember, 'sanctify' means to make holy.)***

- ***Exactly how holy did Paul want God to make his friends?***

Paul wanted every part of these believers to be completely transformed. Every part of their lives was to be made holy.

We are people made up of body, mind and spirit. God cares about what we do with our bodies. He cares about what we do with our minds and hearts too. Every part of us needs to change. Paul prayed that God would do that transforming work in his friends. It was a big ask.

So, twice in this letter Paul has asked God to make his friends holy.

In between these two prayers, Paul has been calling on his friends to make every effort to live holy lives. Paul did not pray that God would make them holy then tell them to just put their feet up and wait for God to do it.

So how does God change us? God works to change us *as* we work hard to obey His Word. The fact that we *do* work hard at obeying God's Word is actually a mark of God being at work in us.

Would these Christians make it? God had called them to belong to Him, to be His holy people. Would they make it?

• ***What reassurance did Paul give these believers in verse 24?***

These believers' hope for the future lay in God's faithfulness and God's power. Paul wanted to remind them of this as he ended his letter. Their hope did not lie in their own strength. God would keep His promises. God would finish the work He had started in them. Paul's friends could face the future with confidence, not because they were great but because they had a great God.

PRAY

• ***Thank God that He is faithful to keep His promises.***

• ***Thank God that He has called you to Himself.***

• ***Thank Him that He is totally committed to making you holy and saving you on the day Jesus returns.***

• ***Pray that you would make every effort to be holy in every area of your life.***

• ***Pray Paul's prayer for Christians you know.***

'Brothers...'

All the way through this letter Paul has been addressing his Christian friends as 'brothers'. It is a lovely way of expressing the love and equality that there is between everyone who is in the Christian family. Everyone, from the newest Christian to the oldest church leader or apostle, was one of the 'brothers'. Brothers love, support and help each other.

Paul closes his letter by calling on his brothers in Thessalonica to do three things for their fellow Christians, their 'brothers'.

- ***What were the three things he wanted them to do?***

Paul has just prayed for these new believers, and now he asks them to pray for him and his co-workers.

What does this tell us? It tells us that there is no such thing as a one-way relationship in the Christian family. Yes, your church leaders should be praying for you. But they need you to pray for them too.

It also tells us that we never graduate from being totally dependent on God.

Paul was an apostle. Silas and Timothy were church leaders. But they knew that they needed God's help all the time. They could not go it alone.

Pray for church leaders you know. Ask God to help you remember your own total dependence on Him too.

The other two things Paul asks them to do refer to 'all the brothers'.

This may mean all the Christians within their fellowship in Thessalonica. It could also mean all the Christians in the area around their city. Either way, Paul wanted them to meet together and to greet each other with warm affection.

This doesn't mean that you have to kiss every single Christian you come across. But we should greet each other in a way which expresses the warmth of brotherly love. We should do that in whatever way is most appropriate in our culture and context.

Pray that you would continue to make meeting with Christians a priority. And that you would treat them with brotherly love.

Lastly, Paul asks these Thessalonian believers to make sure that everyone reads this letter that he has written to them.

He calls on them to do this in the strongest of terms. He says, 'I charge you before the Lord' to do this.

Why was Paul so insistent? Because he knew that he was writing God's words to them (2:13, 4:2). Paul knew that it was through God's words that God's Spirit would keep his friends safe in Christ.

God's word had brought them into the grace of Jesus Christ through the gospel in the first place. God's Word would keep them safe in that grace as they continued to read it and obey it. That was, and is, God's way to keep us safe until Jesus comes.

These Thessalonian Christians had Paul's letter. But some other parts of the New Testament had not yet been written. How privileged we are to be able to read God's completed Word, both Old and New Testaments, to keep us safe in Christ.

Pray that you too would keep reading this letter and the rest of God's Word, the Bible.

• ***How does Paul end his letter?***

When Paul had arrived in their city, he had brought the Thessalonians the news of God's grace. He had told them the message of the death and resurrection of the Lord Jesus Christ. Paul's greatest desire was that his friends should continue in that grace. Pray that you too would do exactly that.

PRAY

• ***Pray for your church leaders.***

• ***Pray that every Christian would remember their total dependence on God.***

• ***Pray that your church fellowship would be full of brotherly love.***

• ***Pray you will continue to make meeting with Christians a priority.***

• ***Pray that you would keep reading and obeying this letter and the rest of the Bible too, so that you stay safe in the grace of Christ.***

Which part of the Bible will you read next? It would be a good idea to ask a Christian friend or your church leader for suggestions. You could also ask for suggestions of good resources to help you as you read. The Bible is God's Word to us, and we need to keep on listening to God.

MORE IN THIS SERIES

MARK: The Suffering Servant *By Jeremy McQuoid*

ISBN: 978-1-906173-55-5

DANIEL: Far From Home *By Justin Mote*

ISBN: 978-1-906173-68-5

ROMANS: Momentous News *By David Cook*

ISBN: 978-1-906173-24-1

10 Publishing
a division of 10ofthose.com

To place an order call: **0844 879 3243** email: **sales@10ofthose.com**
or order online: **www.10ofthose.com**